Biodiversity
of Deserts

GREG PYERS

 **Marshall Cavendish**
Benchmark

New York

This edition first published in 2011 in the United States of America by
MARSHALL CAVENDISH BENCHMARK
An imprint of Marshall Cavendish Corporation

Website: www.marshallcavendish.us

This publication represents the opinions and views of the author based on Greg Pyer's personal experience, knowledge, and research. The information in this book serves as a general guide only. The author and publisher have used their best efforts in preparing this book and disclaim liability rising directly and indirectly from the use and application of this book.

Other Marshall Cavendish Offices:
Marshall Cavendish Ltd. 5th Floor, 32-38 Saffron Hill, London EC1N 8 FH, UK • Marshall Cavendish International (Asia) Private Limited, 1 New Industrial Road, Singapore 536196 • Marshall Cavendish International (Thailand) Co Ltd. 253 Asoke, 12th Flr, Sukhumvit 21 Road, Klongtoey Nua, Wattana, Bangkok 10110, Thailand • Marshall Cavendish (Malaysia) Sdn Bhd, Times Subang, Lot 46, Subang Hi-Tech Industrial Park, Batu Tiga, 40000 Shah Alam, Selangor Darul Ehsan, Malaysia

Marshall Cavendish is a trademark of Times Publishing Limited

All websites were available and accurate when this book was sent to press.

Library of Congress Cataloging-in-Publication Data.
Pyers, Greg.
    Biodiversity of deserts / Greg Pyers.
        p. cm. — (Biodiversity)
    Includes index.
    Summary: "Discusses the variety of living things in a desert ecosystem"—Provided by publisher.
    ISBN 978-1-60870-071-4
    1. Desert biology—Juvenile literature. 2. Desert ecology—Juvenile literature.
    3. Endangered ecosystems—Juvenile literature. I. Title.
    QH88.P94 2010
    577.54—dc22
                                                    2009042313

First published in 2010 by
MACMILLAN EDUCATION AUSTRALIA PTY LTD
15–19 Claremont Street, South Yarra 3141

Visit our website at www.macmillan.com.au or go directly to www.macmillanlibrary.com.au

Associated companies and representatives throughout the world.

Edited by Georgina Garner
Text and cover design by Kerri Wilson
Page layout by Kerri Wilson
Photo research by Legend Images
Illustrations by Richard Morden

Printed in China

Acknowledgments
The author and the publisher are grateful to the following for permission to reproduce copyright material:

Front cover photograph of a perentie hunting near Kata Tjuta, Australia © Danita Delimont/Alamy.
Back cover photograph of a meerkat © EcoPrint/Shutterstock.

Photographs courtesy of:
© Danita Delimont/Alamy, 1; © George H.H. Huey/Alamy, 29; © Michel Gunther-BIOS/AUSCAPE, 19; © D. Parer/E. Parer-Cook/AUSCAPE, 10; © Charles O'Rear/Corbis, 20; Digital Vision/Natphotos, 28; Margo Silver/Getty Images, 23; Photodisc/Jeremy Woodhouse, 21; Photolibrary/Martin Harvey, 17; Photolibrary/Bud Lehnhausen, 7; Photolibrary/Nature's Images, 18; Photolibrary/Kate Thompson, 24; © Anton Foltin/Shutterstock, 13; © Andrzej Gibasiewicz/Shutterstock, 16; © Jhaz Photography/Shutterstock, 22; © N. Frey Photography/Shutterstock, 11; © Alessio Ponti/Shutterstock, 4; USDA/ARS, photo by Peggy Greb, 25.

While every care has been taken to trace and acknowledge copyright, the publisher tenders their apologies for any accidental infringement where copyright has proved untraceable. Where the attempt has been unsuccessful, the publisher welcomes information that would redress the situation.

1 3 5 6 4 2

Contents

Glossary Words

When a word is printed in **bold**, you can look up its meaning in the Glossary on page 31.

What Is Biodiversity?

Biodiversity, or biological diversity, describes the variety of living things in a particular place, in a particular **ecosystem**, or across the entire Earth.

Measuring Biodiversity

The biodiversity of a particular area is measured on three levels:

- **species** diversity, which is the number and variety of species in the area.
- genetic diversity, which is the variety of **genes** each species has. Genes determine the characteristics of different living things. A variety of genes within a species enables it to **adapt** to changes in its environment.
- ecosystem diversity, which is the variety of **habitats** in the area. A diverse ecosystem has many habitats within it.

Species Diversity

Species diversity changes from one habitat to another. Habitats, such as rain forests and deserts, have different levels of biodiversity. Within a desert habitat, lizards live in rocky **outcrops**. Horned vipers and kangaroo rats live in sand. Other animals live in desert grasses.

Habitats and Ecosystems

Deserts are habitats, which are places where animals and plants live. Within a desert habitat, there are also many different types of smaller habitats, sometimes called microhabitats. Some desert microhabitats are sand dunes, stony plains, water holes, cacti and desert grasses, and rocky outcrops. Different kinds of **organisms** live in these places. The animals, plants, other living things, nonliving things, and all the ways they affect each other make up a desert ecosystem.

The biodiversity of Sahara Desert habitats, in Africa, is low.

Biodiversity Under Threat

The variety of species on Earth is under threat. There are somewhere between 5 million and 30 million species on Earth. Most of these species are very small and hard to find, so only about 1.75 million have been described and named. These are called known species.

Scientists estimate that as many as fifty species become **extinct** every day. Extinction is a natural process, but human activities have sped up the rate of extinction by nearly one thousand times.

Known Species of Organisms on Earth

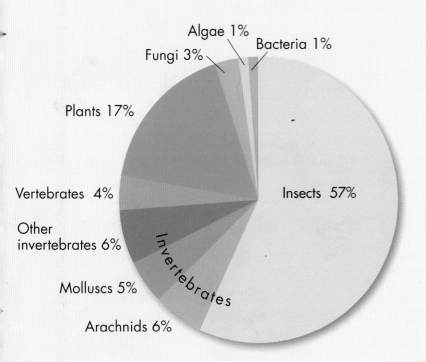

- Algae 1%
- Bacteria 1%
- Fungi 3%
- Plants 17%
- Vertebrates 4%
- Other invertebrates 6%
- Molluscs 5%
- Arachnids 6%
- Insects 57%
- Invertebrates

The known species of organisms on Earth can be divided into bacteria, algae, fungi, plant, and animal species. Animal species are further divided into vertebrates and invertebrates.

Approximate Numbers of Known Vertebrate Species

ANIMAL GROUP	KNOWN SPECIES
Fish	31,000
Birds	10,000
Reptiles	8,800
Amphibians	6,500
Mammals	5,500

Why Is Biodiversity Important?

Biodiversity is important for many reasons. The diverse organisms in an ecosystem take part in natural processes essential to the survival of all living things. Biodiversity produces food and medicine. It is also important to people's quality of life.

Natural Processes

Human survival depends on the natural processes that go on in ecosystems. Through natural processes, air and water is cleaned, waste is decomposed, **nutrients** are recycled, and disease is kept under control. Natural processes depend on the organisms that live in the soil, on the plants that produce oxygen and absorb **carbon dioxide**, and on the organisms that break down dead plants and animals. When species of organisms become extinct, natural processes may stop working.

Food

We depend on biodiversity for our food. The world's major food plants are grains, vegetables, and fruits. These plants have all been bred from plants in the wild. Wild plants are important sources of genes for breeding new disease-resistant crops. If these wild plants were to become extinct, their genes would be lost.

Medicine

About 40 percent of all prescription drugs come from chemicals that have been extracted from plants. Scientists discover new, useful plant chemicals every year. The National Cancer Institute discovered that 70 percent of plants found to have anticancer properties were rain forest plants.

When plant species become extinct, the chemicals within them are lost forever. The lost chemicals might have been important in making new medicines.

Did You Know?

Biodiversity varies over time. Fossils show us that many species of animals and plants that lived in deserts in the past have since become extinct.

Quality of Life

Biodiversity is important to our quality of life. Animals and plants inspire wonder. They are part of our **heritage**. Some species have become particularly important to us. If the blue whale became extinct, our survival would not be affected, but we would feel great sadness and regret.

Extinct Species

The desert rat-kangaroo was a rabbit-sized mammal that lived in stony desert country in inland Australia. It did not shelter from the heat in a burrow. Instead, it built a flimsy grass nest. Little was ever discovered about the desert rat-kangaroo because its habitat was so remote. Cats and foxes introduced to Australia probably preyed on the small mammal. The last time the desert rat-kangaroo was seen was in 1935. The extinction of this and other species is reducing Earth's biodiversity.

Animal species such as blue whales inspire people's wonder and imagination. This improves their quality of life.

7

Deserts of the World

A desert is an area that normally has less than 10 inches (250 millimeters) of **precipitation** each year. Only some plant and animal species can live in these dry conditions. Deserts are found on all the continents except Europe.

Types of Desert

There are many types of desert habitats across the world. Deserts are classified as extremely arid (dry), arid, or semiarid, depending on how much precipitation they get. People usually think of deserts as hot, but there are cold deserts, too, in the polar regions.

Deserts have different physical features. Some deserts have sand dunes, and others have stony ground. Some deserts have cliffs and mountains, and others have vast salt flats.

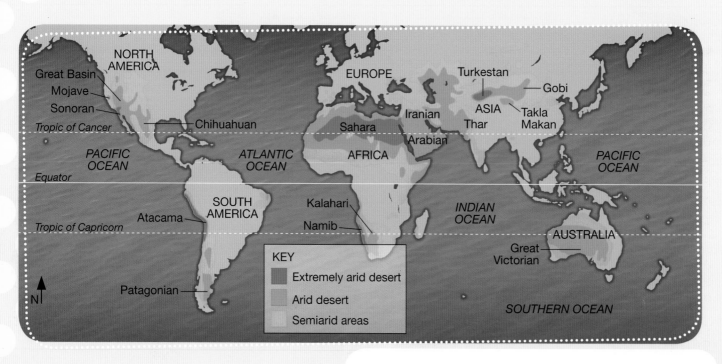

The world's major deserts are located in North America, South America, Africa, Asia, and Australia. Europe has some semiarid areas but no real deserts.

Antarctica

Antarctica is a desert continent. Annual precipitation on the coast is about 7.9 inches (200 mm). Inland, precipitation is less than 2 inches (50 mm). There are no trees or shrubs in Antarctica. No vertebrate animals live entirely on land in Antarctica. All have to go to the sea to feed, or they migrate to other places in winter.

Major Deserts of the World

NAME AND LOCATION	TYPE OF DESERT	PHYSICAL FEATURES				AREA (square miles)
		Sand dunes	Sandy and/or stony plains	Salt flats	Mountains	
Sahara Desert, in northern Africa	Hot	X	X	X	X	3,500,000
Arabian Desert, on the Arabian Peninsula	Hot	X				888,000
Gobi Desert, in northern China and southern Mongolia	Cold		X			465,000
Patagonian Desert, in Argentina	Cold		X			230,000
Turkestan Desert, in central Asia and southwestern Russia	Cold	X				215,000
Chihuahuan Desert, in northern Mexico and the southwestern United States	Hot				X	175,000
Great Basin, in the western United States	Cold		X	X	X	160,000
Great Victorian Desert, in Australia	Hot	X	X			135,000
Takla Makan, in western China	Cold	X				105,000
Sonoran Desert, in the southwestern United States and northern Mexico	Hot		X			85,000
Thar Desert, in India and Pakistan	Hot	X				75,000
Atacama Desert, on the coast of Chile	Cold		X			70,000
Namib Desert, on the coast of southwestern Africa	Hot	X				50,000
Mojave Desert, in the southwestern United States	Hot		X	X		25,000

Desert Biodiversity

Deserts are very dry places. Low precipitation limits plant growth and only a relatively small number of plant species can survive in desert conditions. In turn, this limits the number of animal species that can live in a desert.

A dingo searches for food in the harsh environment of Australia's Sturt Stony Desert.

Desert Animals and Plants

The animals and plants that live in a desert have features that enable them to survive the harsh conditions. They are adapted to their environment.

Because of their adaptations, desert animals and plants are often unlike animals and plants of other habitats. The leaves of many desert plants have waxy surfaces to prevent water loss.

Deserts have a large number of **endemic species**. The protection of deserts is essential to the survival of these species.

Did You Know?

For thousands of years, indigenous Australians burned different patches of desert each year, so that there was a patchwork of **vegetation** at various stages of regrowth. Each patch attracted different kinds of animals for hunting. These fires enriched the desert's biodiversity.

Varied Habitats and Varied Biodiversity

There are different types of deserts and each desert has many types of habitats within it. Desert habitats include sand dunes, stony plains, and cliffs. Deserts may have moist creek beds, scattered water holes, and salt flats. In some deserts, there are even oases, where water is plentiful. Different species of animals and plants have evolved to survive in these different habitats.

Plants and Animals of the Atacama Desert

The Atacama Desert, in Chile, is the driest desert on Earth. In some parts of its 70,000-square-mile (180,000-square-kilometer) area, rain has not fallen for hundreds of years, and the soil is so dry that even **bacteria** cannot live in it. Though very few animal species are found in the Atacama Desert, the biodiversity of the desert is very important. Many of its endemic species are remarkable for being able to survive in some of the world's harshest conditions. Some shrub species survive by collecting moisture from sea fogs that drift in from the Pacific Ocean.

The plants of the Atacama Desert have evolved to survive in its very dry conditions.

Desert Ecosystems

Living and nonliving things, and the **interactions** between them, make up desert ecosystems. Living things are plants and animals. Nonliving things include the rocks, sand, soil, water, wind, sunshine, and frost.

Food Chains and Food Webs

A very important way that different species interact is by eating or consuming other species. This transfers energy and nutrients from one organism to another. A food chain illustrates this flow of energy, by showing what eats what. A food web shows how many different food chains fit together.

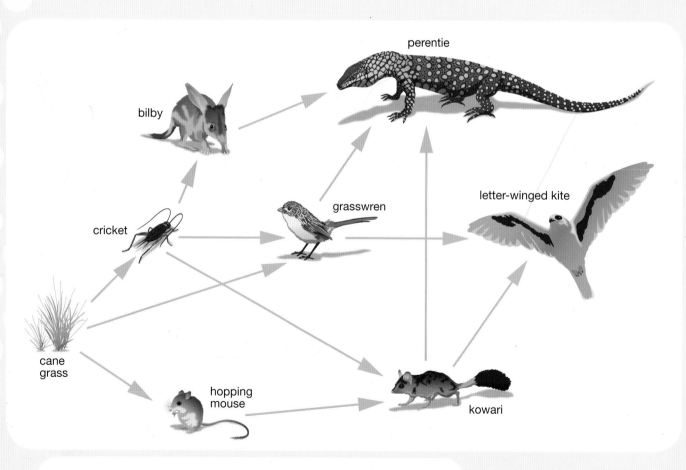

perentie

bilby

cricket

grasswren

letter-winged kite

cane grass

hopping mouse

kowari

This Australian desert food web is made up of several food chains. In one food chain, cane grass is eaten by grasswrens, which in turn are eaten by perenties.

Other Interactions

Nonliving things and living things in a desert interact in other ways, too. Where the soil is soft, desert animals such as kangaroo rats dig burrows to escape the heat of the day. Snakes often use the burrows of small desert mammals to shelter from the midday heat. Larger animals, such as gazelles or coyotes, find shade beneath acacia trees or cacti, or among rocks.

Desert Rainfall

Rainfall is scarce in a desert but every ten years or so there may be a heavy fall of rain, called a deluge. Seeds that have lain dormant, or inactive, in the soil sprout and the desert is soon carpeted in wildflowers.

Animals, too, respond to the heavy rain. Frogs that have buried themselves deep in the soil emerge to breed, and fish swim out from their desert pools to find new pools. Animals take advantage of the plant growth. In Australia's Simpson Desert, different kinds of birds arrive to feast on seeds.

Couch's Spadefoot Toad

Couch's spadefoot toad is native to the Sonoran Desert, in Mexico and the United States. It survives the dry desert **climate** by spending up to ten months of the year 3 feet (1 meter) underground. It digs its own burrow or uses the burrows of kangaroo rats. When it rains, the spadefoot toad comes to the surface, mates, and lays eggs. These hatch in nine hours and the tadpoles become adults in about ten days.

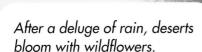
After a deluge of rain, deserts bloom with wildflowers.

Threats to Desert Biodiversity

Deserts are often thought of as wastelands. This attitude has meant that deserts and their biodiversity have not been given as much protection as they need. Today, the biodiversity of many deserts faces a range of threats.

Biodiversity Hotspots

A biodiversity hotspot is an area that has a high number of endemic species and biodiversity that is still mainly intact, but this biodiversity is under threat. Threats to biodiversity hotspots come from such things as agricultural and **urban** development, the wildlife trade, and pollution.

Throughout the world, there are only two biodiversity hotspots that are entirely desert. These hotspots are the Horn of Africa in northeastern Africa and the Succulent Karoo of southwestern Africa.

Species of the Succulent Karoo and the Horn of Africa

SPECIES GROUP	SUCCULENT KAROO		HORN OF AFRICA	
	Total number of species	Number of endemic species	Total number of species	Number of endemic species
Plants	6,356	2,439	5,000	2,750
Mammals	75	2	220	20
Birds	226	1	697	24
Reptiles	94	15	285	93
Amphibians	21	1	30	6
Freshwater fish	28	0	100	10

Halfmens

The halfmens is a very strange **succulent** plant of the Succulent Karoo. It is called the halfmens because from a distance it looks like a person walking up a hill. The plant grows to about 13 feet (4 m) high and has a stem that resembles an elephant's trunk, so it is also called elephant's trunk.

Human Threats to Biodiversity Hotspots

Only 300,000 people live in the Succulent Karoo hotspot. That is just nine people per square mile, so human population pressure is not a serious threat to the region's biodiversity. Major threats to the hotspot are mining, overgrazing, plant stealing, and farming.

In the Horn of Africa, however, the population density is around sixty people per square mile. This many people places great pressure on the region's biodiversity. Only 5 percent of the region's original vegetation remains due to firewood collection and overgrazing by domestic animals. Major threats to the hotspot are overgrazing, war, hunting, and wood collection for making charcoal.

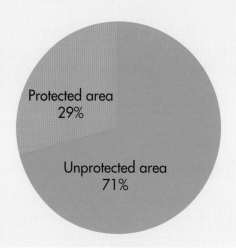

The Succulent Karoo hotspot covers a total area of 39,000 square miles (102,000 sq km).

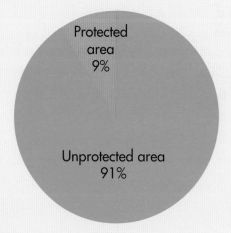

The Horn of Africa hotspot covers a total area of 643,000 square miles (1,666,000 sq km).

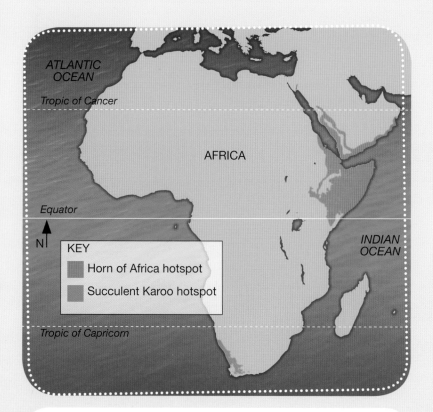

Both desert biodiversity hotspots are in Africa.

BIODIVERSITY THREAT:
Grazing Animals and Invasive Species

Animals such as cattle, sheep, and goats wander over large areas of desert and graze on the best plants. These and other **invasive species** alter the desert ecosystem and threaten biodiversity.

Grazing

Farm animals are often allowed to graze over large areas of desert. Over time, this changes the biodiversity of these areas. Grasses are eaten by sheep and cattle. Goats eat the leaves and strip the bark off shrubs, which may not survive. The desert animals that live in or on those grasses or shrubs lose their habitat. Cattle, goats, and sheep have hard hooves, which break up the desert soil as they walk across it. The soil blows away, taking with it valuable nutrients needed by desert plants. Heavy cattle also trample the burrows of desert animals.

Invasive Plants

Invasive plants are plants that are brought to an area, thrive in their new home, and become environmental weeds. These species may overwhelm local species, and some local species may disappear altogether from certain areas. Tamarisk, also called salt cedar, is a northern African tree that was introduced into Australia and the United States. It spread rapidly along desert watercourses, taking over native vegetation.

Tamarisk trees have spread through desert habitats in Utah.

Invasive Animals in Australia's Deserts

In the last two hundred years, about half of the world's mammal extinctions have occurred in Australia. Most of these were small-sized to medium-sized desert mammals. The main causes of these extinctions are the European red fox and the **feral** cat. These introduced and invasive species prey on small- to medium-sized mammals.

The European rabbit is another nonnative species. It grazes heavily on desert plants. Where rabbits have been controlled, many plant species have reappeared, growing from seeds in the desert soil. Feral horses and donkeys roam desert regions of Australia, too. They graze on desert plants and their hard hooves turn desert soil to dust.

The mala of Australia's Tanami Desert is hunted by invasive animals such as cats and foxes.

Did You Know?

As many as one million camels roam wild across Australia's deserts. These animals descended from camels brought to Australia by explorers in the 1800s. A herd of camels can drink a desert water hole dry, leaving no water for native wildlife.

BIODIVERSITY THREAT:
Wildlife Trade and Hunting

Desert plants and animals are taken illegally by **poachers** and sold in the wildlife trade. Other desert animal species are hunted by people for food.

Pet Trade

The Egyptian tortoise is among the world's most endangered tortoises, mainly because of the illegal pet trade. It is no longer found in Egypt and populations are small in Israel and Libya. Males grow to just 5 inches (12 centimeters) and females grow to 3.5 inches (9 cm). Many people want Egyptian tortoises as pets. When they buy one from a pet shop, however, they do not know that the tortoise they have bought may have been caught illegally in the wild.

The Egyptian tortoise is one of the world's smallest tortoises and is popular as a pet.

Nursery Trade

Desert plants are popular additions to many gardens. Many desert plants sold in plant nurseries have been taken illegally from the wild. In Mexico and the United States, many species of cacti are dug up in the Chihuahuan Desert for sale in city nurseries. In Africa, succulent plants of many kinds are removed from deserts in the Horn of Africa and the Succulent Karoo and sold as far away as Europe.

Did You Know?

Stealing plants is a major threat to biodiversity and the effects are long lasting. The saguaro cactus takes one hundred years to grow just 6.5 feet (2 m) tall, so it takes a very long time to be replaced.

Hunting

Scimitar-horned oryx, Arabian oryx, and addax are desert antelopes. Desert people have hunted these animals for their meat and skins for thousands of years. The animals' impressive horns are highly prized, too. When cars and rifles became available to desert people, many more of these animals were killed. In 1972, the Arabian oryx became extinct in the wild. The scimitar-horned oryx is also thought to be extinct in the wild. Addax survive only in isolated areas of the Sahara Desert.

The Effects of War

War in Somalia and other parts of the Horn of Africa has had serious consequences for desert biodiversity. Many animals, especially large plant-eating animals, are hunted for meat. Ibex, oryx, gazelles, and zebras are among the animals most affected. War disrupts where animals can roam, and government responsibilities such as wildlife protection are neglected.

In 1982 Arabian oryx were reintroduced into the wild, in Oman, from a herd bred from captive animals. These animals had been extinct in the wild for ten years, due to hunting.

BIODIVERSITY THREAT:
Mining, Farming, and Building Roads

Mining, agricultural activities, and the construction of roads change the habitat of many desert species. Mining destroys desert habitats, farming takes water from deserts, and roads disrupt and disturb wildlife.

Mining

A lot of mining takes place in deserts around the world. Mining involves disturbing the ground to remove the minerals beneath it. As a result, vegetation is destroyed. Almost all of the Succulent Karoo coastline, in Africa, has been mined for diamonds. There is also mining for marble, titanium, and other minerals.

Mines affect biodiversity and so do other activities associated with mining. Mining employees' four-wheel drives are a major threat to the gravel plains of the Namib Desert, in southern Africa. These vehicles damage slow-growing desert plants, which take years to recover.

Farming

Crops grown in desert regions require **irrigation**. Irrigation takes water from other areas and reduces the amount of water available for the desert habitat, sometimes by huge amounts. In the Chihuahuan and Sonoran desert regions of the United States and Mexico, water is scarce. Up to 90 percent of the water of the Rio Grande, which flows through the Chihuahuan Desert, is diverted for irrigation. In 2001, this river dried up altogether.

Damming Desert Rivers

In the Succulent Karoo of southwestern Africa, grapes, citrus fruits, tobacco, and vegetable crops are grown on farms. These crops are irrigated using water collected from dams that have been constructed on rivers in the region. Damming the rivers changes the water cycle and the desert ecosystem. More dams are proposed in the Succulent Karoo. This could mean trouble for the native species.

A desert in South Africa is mined for diamonds.

Roads

Roads break up a desert, cutting off one area of habitat from another. This is called habitat fragmentation.

A road built through a desert affects desert wildlife in several ways. It:

- is a physical barrier to animal movement
- is a danger to the animals that do cross it
- separates populations of the same species, increasing **inbreeding**, and so limits genetic diversity in a species
- allows vehicles bringing invasive species to enter the desert
- makes it easier for poachers and hunters to get into the desert.

Roads passing through deserts bring invasive species, poachers, cars, and trucks, all of which endanger local species.

Disappearing Wilderness Areas

A desert wilderness area is a remote area of desert, more than 3.1 miles (5 km) from any road or building, where there are no signs of human activity. Desert wilderness areas are essential to the continuing **evolution** of desert biodiversity, free of human disturbance. Scientists predict that with roads, towns, and grazing pressures, wilderness areas may decline from 59 percent of total desert area in 2005 to between 31 and 44 percent by 2050.

BIODIVERSITY THREAT:
Climate Change

The world's average temperature is rising, in a process known as global warming. Global warming results in climate changes, such as reduced rainfall in deserts and an increasing number of desert fires. This climate change has consequences for desert biodiversity.

Global Warming

Levels of certain gases, such as carbon dioxide, are increasing in Earth's atmosphere. These gases, called greenhouse gases, trap heat in the atmosphere, as glass does in a greenhouse. The overall increase in temperature, called global warming, is causing changes to Earth's climate. These changes are affecting deserts.

Reduced Rainfall

Desert plants and animals live in a habitat where rainfall is already very scarce. If desert rainfall declines any further, due to climate change, many species may not be able to survive. If rainfall in the grassland and woodland habitats surrounding deserts declines, new desert habitat will form. Desert species may be able to move into these areas.

Desert Fish Migration

In many deserts, fish are confined to water holes for years at a time. Every ten years or so, heavy rains bring floods. The fish breed and spread out across the flooded land. If climate change means that the water holes dry up or that periodic flooding occurs less often or does not occur at all, many desert fish species will face extinction.

Rain is rare in the desert, and climate change may make it even rarer.

Desert plants begin to regrow after a desert fire in California. More desert fires are expected as Earth gets warmer.

More Fires

Rising temperatures are likely to increase the number and intensity of desert fires. Fires kill trees and shrubs, but grasses regrow soon after being burned. In time, an increase in the number of fires would change desert biodiversity. Trees and shrubs would be replaced by grasses. Animals that feed on or shelter in trees or shrubs would lose their habitat. Those species that live among the grasses or eat grass seeds may increase in number.

Did You Know?

In a study conducted between 1975 and 2000, scientists found the average temperature increased in nine out of twelve studied deserts. From these findings, scientists predict average temperature in all deserts will increase by between 1.8 and 12.6 degrees Fahrenheit (1 and 7 degrees Celsius) by 2100.

Desert Conservation

Conservation is the protection, preservation, and wise use of resources and habitats, such as deserts. Some human activities threaten desert biodiversity and cause conservation problems. Research, education, and the establishment of desert reserves can help conserve desert biodiversity.

Conservation Problems

Human threats are changing desert biodiversity. Scientists have predicted that in the Chihuahuan Desert, half of the bird, mammal, and butterfly species will be replaced by other species by 2055. Conservation will help prevent this loss of biodiversity.

Research

Research surveys or studies are used to find out information about deserts, such as how desert ecosystems work and how humans affect them. Research helps people find ways to conserve desert biodiversity. Studies are carried out by scientists, many of whom work for governments and conservation organizations. Naturalists, who are people who study nature as volunteers, also help collect information and data.

A biologist tries to catch a lizard while researching the biodiversity of a desert area.

Desert Soils Store Carbon

Research has shown that bacteria in desert soil take carbon dioxide from the air and convert it to **humus**. This enriches the soil for plant growth and reduces the amount of carbon dioxide in the atmosphere.

Desert Tortoise Decision

In 2001 a Californian court ruled that cattle grazing was no longer allowed on 770 square miles (2,000 sq km) of the Mojave Desert in California. This decision was made to protect the endangered desert tortoise. Cattle trample this animal and its burrows and eat the plants it feeds on.

Desert Reserves

Setting aside areas of deserts as national parks and other reserves is important. These areas need to be managed so that invasive species do not spread and so that illegal activities, such as wildlife poaching, are prevented. Only a very small proportion of the world's deserts is protected in reserves.

A group of children are taught how to conserve desert plants in the Chihuahua Desert in Mexico.

Education

Educating people about desert conservation is very important. People who live in desert areas are often taught how to grow gardens that do not need much water. They are also taught not to use plants that may become environmental weeds in the desert. Schools and organizations such as the Arizona–Sonora Desert Museum in Tucson, Arizona, educate people about living harmoniously with the desert environment.

CASE STUDY:
The Sonoran Desert

The Sonoran Desert of the southwestern United States and northern Mexico covers about 85,000 square miles (220,000 sq km). It has many habitat types and climates. Many organizations are working to protect its biodiversity from threats.

Biodiversity of the Desert

The Sonoran Desert has many habitats, such as sand dunes, rocky plateaus, and mountains. The climate varies across the desert. Some parts have annual rainfall of up to 12 inches (300 mm) a year. In the driest parts of the desert, there is just 3.5 inches (90 mm) of annual rainfall. With such a diverse range of habitats and climate, the Sonoran Desert has among the richest biodiversity of any desert.

Species of the Sonoran Desert

SPECIES GROUP	NUMBER OF SPECIES	EXAMPLE OF SPECIES
Plants	560	Includes the creosote bush and saguaro cactus, which is the world's largest cactus
Birds	261	Includes the roadrunner, several hummingbird species, and two endemic species
Mammals	60	Includes the pronghorn antelope, desert bighorn sheep, puma, and ring-tailed cat
Reptiles	58	Includes six rattlesnake species and the gila monster, which is one of the world's two types of venomous lizards
Fish	About 30	Includes the longfin dace and speckled dace
Amphibians	About 12	Includes the tiger salamander, which is the world's largest land-based salamander

Nutrient-rich Areas

Legumes are plants that take nitrogen gas from the air and make nitrates, which are nutrients that enrich the soil and help plant growth. Places in the Sonoran Desert where legumes, such as ironwood and palo verde, grow are also home to a variety of other plant species. A great variety of other plant species also grows.

Threats to Biodiversity

Sonoran Desert biodiversity is threatened by many human activities. The cities of Phoenix and Tucson, Arizona, are growing. **Urbanization** results in housing developments replacing the habitats of desert animals such as bighorn sheep and pronghorn antelope. Other threats include:

- farming and agriculture, which has spread along the rivers that flow through the region. Farms take water from the desert rivers, reducing the amount available for desert habitats.

- off-road driving, which does serious damage to desert vegetation

- trophy hunting, which is hunting large animals for fun. In Mexico, bighorn sheep are shot by hunters who pay large sums to landowners.

Buffel Grass

Buffel grass was introduced into the Sonoran Desert region from Africa. It was estrablished as grass for grazing cattle. Buffel grass forms dense patches that burn easily and result in fires so hot that ironwood and other native plants are killed. The buffel grass survives the fire. Over time, the desert scrub becomes dominated by buffel grass, threatening biodiversity.

The Sonoran Desert spreads across California and Arizona, in the United States, and Baja California and Sonora, in Mexico.

Alaska

Canada

PACIFIC OCEAN

KEY
Sonoran Desert area

United States

ATLANTIC OCEAN

N

Tropic of Cancer

Mexico

Protecting the Sonoran Desert

Protection of the remaining areas of the Sonoran Desert is very important. Farming, grazing, and urbanization have already altered about 60 percent of the United States' area of the desert.

National Parks

Only about 17 percent of the United States' part of the Sonoran Desert is protected in national parks. Four new parks have been established on the Mexican side of the desert. Altogether, these reserves form the largest area of protected desert in North America.

The national park areas, however, do not connect to other protected areas. This means that wildlife may become isolated in certain areas, unable to migrate across the whole desert. Already, highways are a major barrier to the movement of some species, such as toads and lizards.

Coalition for Sonoran Desert Protection

The Coalition for Sonoran Desert Protection is a community organization of 30,000 people in Tucson, Arizona. The group is committed to "the conservation of biological diversity and ecological function of the Sonoran Desert." The coalition and government created the Sonoran Desert Conservation Plan, which provides guidelines for development so that construction projects will minimally impact the environment.

More plant species live in the Sonoran Desert than in any other desert, but only some parts of the desert are protected as national parks and reserves.

Research and Education

Research and education are vital to the conservation of the Sonoran Desert. Several organizations are involved in educating schools, the public, and tourists:

- The Center for Sonoran Desert Studies at the Arizona–Sonora Desert Museum conducts research into desert biodiversity and provides educational material for schools and the public

- The Sonoran Desert Research Station at Tuscon, Arizona, is run by the United States Geological Survey and the University of Arizona. It carries out research into desert ecosystems and provides information to farmers and local governments about how to protect desert biodiversity.

- The Sonoran Desert Coastal Conservation is a nonprofit conservation organization. It works to establish new reserves in the Mexican Sonoran Desert. These reserves will be positioned so that all habitat types in the desert will be protected.

Did You Know?

In 2007, more than two hundred fines were issued in Arizona to people who illegally took plants from the Sonoran Desert. The desert has 227 protected plant species. Desert plants, including many cacti, can sell for thousands of dollars.

A scientist at the Arizona–Sonora Desert Museum describes the flight patterns and behavior of a desert barn owl.

What Is the Future of Deserts?

Scientists predict that in the future rainfall will increase in some deserts, such as the Gobi, but decline in others, such as the Sahara. These changes will affect biodiversity. Some desert species will thrive, and other species will disappear.

What Can You Do For Deserts?

You can help protect deserts in several ways:

- Find out about deserts. Why are they important and what threatens them?
- Become a responsible consumer. Do not litter, do not waste water, and choose plants for your garden that will not harm native plants.
- If you are concerned about deserts in your area, or in other areas, send a letter to or e-mail your local newspaper, your state congressperson, or local representative, and express your concerns. Know what you want to say, set out your argument, be sure of your facts, and ask for a reply.

Useful Websites

www.desertmuseum.org/kids
The Arizona–Sonora Desert Museum website has fact sheets on the Sonoran Desert and its animal and plant species.

www.biodiversityhotspots.org
This website has information about the richest and most threatened areas of biodiversity on Earth.

www.iucnredlist.org
The International Union for Conservation of Nature (IUCN) Red List has information about threatened plant and animal species.

Glossary

adapt   Change in order to survive.

bacteria   Types of single-celled microscopic organisms.

carbon dioxide   A colorless and odorless gas produced by plants, animals, and the burning of coal and oil.

climate   The weather conditions in a certain region over a long period of time.

ecosystem   The living and nonliving things in a certain area and the interactions between them.

endemic species   Species found only in a particular area.

evolution   Process by which species change.

extinct   Having no living members.

feral   Wild, especially domestic animals that have gone wild.

genes   Segments of deoxyribonucleic acid (DNA) in the cells of a living thing, which determine characteristics.

habitats   Places where animals, plants, or other living things live.

heritage   Things we inherit and pass on to future generations.

humus   The material in soil that comes from living things.

inbreeding   Breeding with closely related individuals so that certain traits are more common and others disappear.

interactions   Actions that are taken together or that affect each other.

invasive species   Nonnative species that negatively affect their new habitats.

irrigation   The supply of water to crops.

nutrients   Substances that are used by living things for growth.

organisms   Animals, plants, and other living things.

outcrops   Rock formations that are visible above the ground.

poachers   People who hunt or take wildlife illegally.

precipitation   Rain, snow, hail, or sleet that falls to the ground.

species   A group of animals, plants, or other living things that share the same characteristics and can breed with one another.

succulent   Type of plant that has adapted to dry conditions, with a stem or fleshy leaves that can store water.

urban   Of towns and cities.

urbanization   The development of towns and cities.

vegetation   Plants.

Index